HOPE my light in the darkness

Sharon Tobler

BookLeaf
Publishing

India | USA | UK

Presentation by *BookLeaf Publishing*

Web: www.bookleafpub.com

E-mail: info@bookleafpub.com

ISBN:9789358314281

First edition 2024

DEDICATION

Dedicated to my family and friends who have come on this literary adventure with me. Your belief, encouragement, insights and wisdom have been invaluable. I am so grateful to you all. I love you deeply.

Trust your instincts and let the creativity flow and don't get to the end wondering!

Ripples

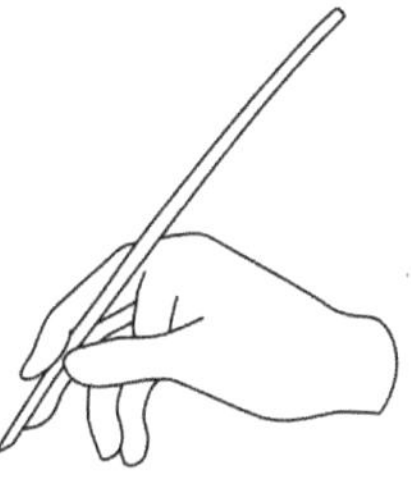

There are ripples left from what's gone before
The canvas is blank, but desiring more
No boundaries marked, no lines in keeping
The lessons learned are ready for reaping.

Go with it now, there is nothing to lose
A colourful palette of words to choose
Reflections, scenes, experiences will
His whispering voice, your heart to fill.

Places been, opportunities taken
He knows what's ahead
This treasure you'll find, O blessed daughter
You are the canvas, he is the author.

What's in your Hands?

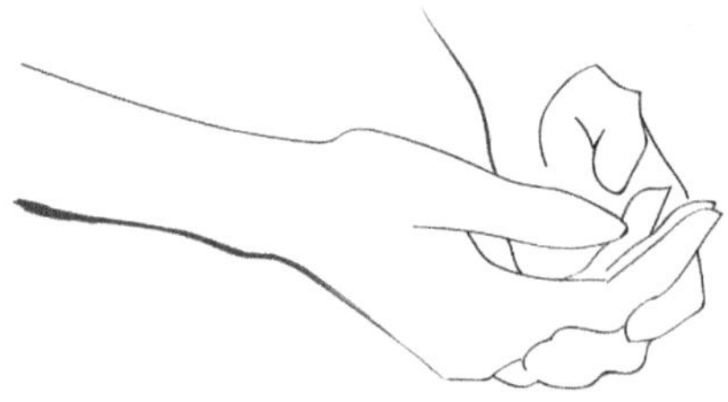

These words I've heard echoed through time
'What's in your hands?'
I look down and think
'Do you mean mine?'

Well, sometimes it's a whistle, a ball and the like
A brush, a paddle, handlebars of a bike.
How can they be useful?
It doesn't seem much!

'Use them' I hear
New pathways you'll see
And as you move forward
It will become clearer.

You've got something special
Gifts from above
Your smile, two hands
And a heart full of love.

So use these for others
As small as it seems
And as you do,
Remember to do it for me.

Where I grow

When I'm not quite sure what to do
I'm reminded 'Go to where you grow'
So I head straight away to those spaces
Where nature's beauty is on show.

Away from the hustle and bustle
The distractions of everyday life
To the places where I can stop and listen
Be still and feel so alive.

These wonderful places you show me
Of quietness, peace and calm
Where I can sit, look and listen
Evidence of a creative hand.

The water is still and clear
Birds softly call
A gentle breeze comes over my shoulder
Making the leaves gracefully fall.

Grasses and flowers vibrate
As the wind continues to weave
Along the creek and through the trees
Then slowly disappears.

Cicadas start in unison with their distinctive
noise
Rising up in a crescendo
Then fading to quiet once more.

I'm grateful for these refresh times
To re-centre my scattered senses
It's like applying a soothing balm
Helps me to live as I'm meant to.

Seasons

In life there are seasons
And not always just one at a time
Of only good or only bad
We tend to have a mixture at times.

On our incredibly good days,
We can know hardships too
And even on the very worst of days
There will be gems and good things too.

There seems to be a false promise
That we can live a trouble-free life
Exempt from hardship and crisis
We just have to 'do everything right!'

Yet, previous generations would attest
That through the tough times and challenges of
life

They grew their faith and forged the grit that
built their determination, strength and might.

A problem-free life would leave us weak
Our character underdeveloped
To grow the qualities of perseverance,
persistence and endurance
Come from pushing through and intentional
habits.

As we are not promised a trouble-free life
We need to reframe the view.
To stop, pause, take a look
Our response is what we get to choose.

Some of the challenges and chaos we experience
The cutting back, pruning, reshaping
Will turn out to be
The sources of opportunity for renewal, and
creativity.

Don't despise the small beginnings
Or be discouraged by baby steps
The seasons of walking through the challenges
in life
Will be linked to our greatest growth.

A better me

'Can you pray for me?' I hear my friend say
It's getting too uncomfortable to stay this way
I want to move on and get out of this place
Away from where the constant battle is waged.

I've walked both morn and evening
Read the Word and journaled my thoughts
Headed off into the day feeling ok
But deep inside I know there is much more.

I set myself some big challenges
Breakthroughs on a whole range of fronts
In order to be the best version of me
To get out of this emotional slump.

'I feel like … I need… I've been…'
STOP… it's time to explore within
Shine a discerning light deep into the crevices
And get to the crux of this thing.

Mentally it's going to be hard
Been a while veiled away in this place
It will take a skilled surgeon and radical surgery
To release the bitterness, hurt and pain.

There will be a wound and tenderness
In the parts where the surgery is performed
It will take time to heal, yes there will be tears
And ultimately scars will form.

The reconstruction will happen slowly
There are steps along the path
In order for this to be a permanent change
For a healthy new self to last.

The scars will be a part of your story
There will be a freshness and so much more
room
Your life will overflow
As you spectacularly bloom.

He is with you

Bring it before God, I hear someone say.
It's OK to pour out your heart this way.
When you're sad, confused and feeling alone.
Talk to him like you would on a phone.

In your disappointments and sorrows, He is with
you.
When all you want is a 'please explain!'
He gives you promises to cling on to
It's not time to withdraw or turn away.

He understands and knows the roads you travel
He's been here and experienced it all
Been misunderstood, mistreated, rejected
While He demonstrated His love for us all.

He knows there is much to gain though this
season
Continues to stand with you right where you are
Embraces, shields and protects you
While He sustains you and guides your path.

The garden of my mind

In the garden of my mind
I have the opportunity
To grow the gift you have given me
To feed and nurture the creativity
The thoughts and patterns that will help or
hinder me.

To water and nourish
To weed and to tend
Will help determine how this garden will fair in
the end.

It's a labour of love, the beautiful mind
It will come at a cost and the sacrifice of time
With gentleness, patience and being kind
To see how it shapes and thrives over time.

This mind will flourish and bloom
extraordinarily
The growth and its fruits
Will be the evidence you see
Of a garden well-loved
With its roots deep and free.

God speaks

My ways and not your ways
Let me be clear
There is a bigger picture unfolding
Things you cannot see from here.

This journey has lives and futures at stake
Eternity is the goal, don't make the mistake
Of not seeing further ahead, for yourself and
today
There is so much more, just keep showing the
way.

There are people I will bring in close for a bit
To be cared for and nurtured, their light to be lit
Guide, encourage and build them up for the day
Then they will be ready to continue on their
way.

So keep the main thing the main thing
Daily walk close to me
Hear my voice and enjoy fellowship sweet
Until the day face-to-face we meet.

Be who you are

Be who you are.
Bravely step into the new
You know where you have to start
This is uniquely shaped for you.

Be fearless in this new pursuit
Of things that set your soul on fire
You'll see it is a perfect fit
Bespoke and lightweight too.

To be where you are right now
For such a time as this
There are some divine appointments
That you will not want to miss.

You are stronger than you think
The message is loud and clear
And don't forget who's on your side
And who is always very near.

So step out into these places
Knowing the hard things you can do
To forgive, show love and kindness
Live a life that is renewed.

There is a world out there just waiting
People's lives in such turmoil
Looking for hope and a pathway through
To find true peace and joy.

Be beautiful and shine your light
For all the world to see
Even a damaged broken life
He can use for His glory.

This story

Standing at the edge of now
Viewing all that has been
With tears welling up my eyes
I survey the scene.

There is beauty and there is ash.
Dreams lost and hopes scattered
The promise of a better future
Is more than I can imagine.

The same God who was writing my story then
Is still writing this story now
He brings beauty and healing
From all the brokenness somehow.

He is still here with me
My ever, faithful friend
He loves and holds onto me
As I trust Him to the end.

There is a red sea before me
He calls me to step in
Bravely into the deeper waters
To places I've never been.

He's got me in His hand
Every step of the way
To be brave and fearless
And obediently walk His way.

Lord, can I trust you?

There were some things in life Lord
I never dreamed I would lose
Was left feeling rejected, broken and bruised.

Life seemed so marred
So painfully torn
The reminders and memories daily I mourned.

A heart so broken
So what's left of me?
A vessel so damaged, yet useful maybe?

But You say to trust You
You'll carry me through
There is something—a new life much better,
walking closer to You.

You promise to be here all my days through
To heal, to hold me
To guide my way too.

So here I stand Lord, surrendered to You
With this hope in my heart, and in Your
goodness too.
For the pathways ahead and the spectacular
views.
Yes Lord I know, I can trust You.

A trusted friend

Who do you have in your life
That walks close alongside
Believes and sees the best in you
Speaks truth and inspires.

Shares in life's hopes and challenges
A voice to speak into you
So you're authentic and accountable
And become a better version of you.

Loves you when you're not so lovable
Shows you mercy and gritty grace
A spiritual gate keeper and guide
Connecting you with the how and why.

With whom you can really be you
Feel understood, valued and heard

Lifts you up and invites you to grow
Passing on the insights they've learned.

Be brave and have these people around you
To connect and cheer you on
Through all of life's different seasons
So you can flourish and shine.

Transitions

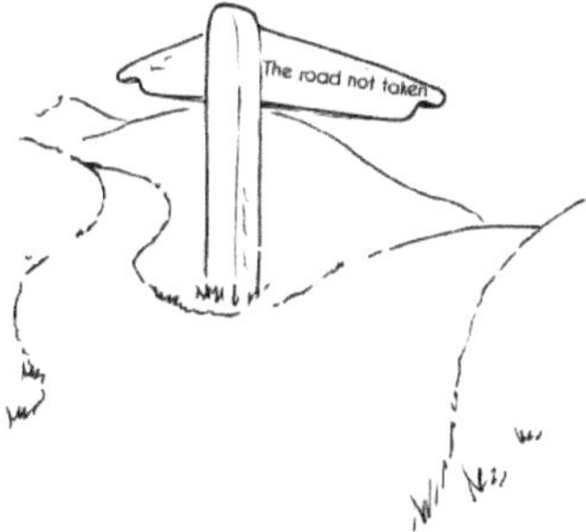

'Transitions…'
Oh! I hope my resilience is ready to bounce
They can come with a warning
Or show up unannounced.

It's that place in between
Heading from here to there
Waiting, wondering, preparing
Contemplating, what is next?

How do we get 'there'?
What are the steps?
The process, procedures
The navigating through to the next.

God, when You called out Abram to leave his
place
You just spoke Your words

No details You gave.

So is this the same?
This journey we're on,
A walk of trust and obedience
Into the new and beyond.

You lead and guide us through to a better way
Tomorrows and a future we could never create
Bigger, bolder, brighter days than we could have
thought possible
While stumbling in the haze.

A life full of colour, wonder and awe.
Awaits us beyond the transition door
Catch a glimpse and be assured
There is going to be so much more.

Simply be still and wait

Sitting in the still… in the still places
Simply be still and wait
To receive the promise from God in His time
Simply be still and wait.

He provides hope in this time of waiting
Builds perseverance to endure
As we sit and it feels as if nothing is happening
It is crucial that we stay still.

In the still it's time to be faithful
Rather than attempting to hasten the pace
This still place is important
Where God gives us the promise before he gives
us the way.

In the still place we learn to identify God's voice
And in His silence is where our faith is exhibited

Lessons are learned from these times
Of strength, patience and obedience.

Don't compromise your promise
By refusing to wait on God in the still place
Allow Him to complete his work in and for you.
Simply be still and wait.

Reframing

'This is not the way life was supposed to be'
Has been the cry of many
But be assured God has a plan
To complete what He has started already.

The message is still the same
This is not the time to hide
He uses us just where we are
Walking side by side.

Building confidence as we trust
We are called to be salt and light
To walk humbly without fear
Keeping our eyes on the prize.

We cannot control what happens
Take time to reframe it in our mind

To get more perspective
For a better response to find.

A constant stream of people
Drawing alongside
With whom to have conversations
To encourage and guide.

God is moving
In the midst of the unexpected
So take time to reframe the view
And be prepared to be more deeply connected.

Letting go

Letting go of the familiar
The things you've come to know
The fine threads created to hold you here
Will start to disconnect and let you go.

The surroundings, the smells and the sounds
That have become so familiar 'til now
Will be the gems in your mind
To take with you as you journey away.

The feel, the people, the deep connections
Things so special to this season
Will not be lost, but will live on
As treasures and stories for safekeeping.

Surrender

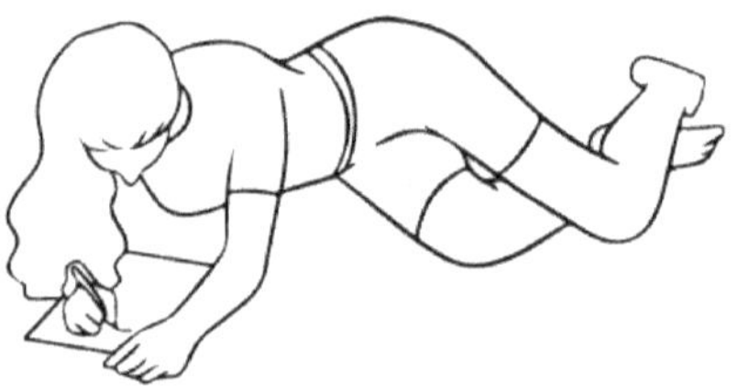

When the fog is obstructing my view
Painfully aware of my faults and my flaws
I ask how can you use me
I don't feel like I am enough at all.

But You tell me Fear Not!
It is in my weakness You do Your best work
It's when You can use me the most
In ways that will get Your message heard.

So trusting the words of the One who loves me
Knowing the reliability of what's gone before
To find strength, words and clarity
I surrender to the process once more.

The journey is not a quick makeover
There are layers and restoring to do
At times it is so painfully slow
But the rebuild is making all things new.

With another blank page before me
I know I'm not doing this all on my own
With the promise that You are here with me
I'll continue to make Your story known.

Love

Love
Love well
Love in the places when it's easy
Love in the places when it's hard

Love
Love you
Love me
Love God

Love
Love when you're young
Love when you're old
Love when it's near the end

Love
Love when there is love returned
Love when there is no love
Love when it hurts

Love
Love when you understand it
Love when you don't
Love when you're sitting in a giant pause.

Love and grace

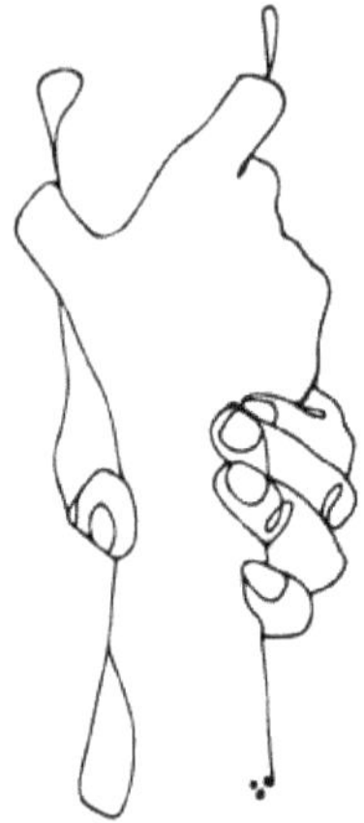

Love, You have found us
Grace upon Grace You have poured on us
Your face you did not turn away
Even through our troubled times
When we think we are too far gone
You are there to guide the way.

You hold our hands in the darkness
Show us our true worth
Love sees us right where we are
You never quit but pursue us
Ready to forgive and renew us
We are never too far away.

The broken are fully renewed
Simply come just as you

There is never too much shame or disgrace
A new life is available to you
Love is right here for you
Ever faithful and won't let you down.

Hope… my light in darkness

In the darkness a small light stands out
It needs to be nurtured to shine without faltering
One light alone is vulnerable
Many lights together are too strong to
extinguish.

I was one light in the dark place
Stumbling, lost, when I saw a light ahead in the
tunnel
I headed for it and quickly realised that I was
being a light
Shining for others to follow on their dark
journey.

In times of darkness we offer hope,
encouragement, kindness, compassion
When others are struggling we help show the
way
So others regain their glow and shine
And see the good and the beautiful in life again.

Be light at home, at school, in the workplace and
the community
Shine in order to help others
So they can reimagine their lives
And point them to the One who strengthens us to
do this
So we know who we truly are and can live life in
all its fullness.

A modern-day Ruth

A modern-day Ruth with her virtues to see
An honourable pursuit for this world that is in
need
Choosing kindness even when others choose not
to be
Daily she chooses to have a gentle spirit, to
walk, and to pray
Because that's what she has been shown along
the way.

Grace and mercy her Heavenly Father lovingly
displays
Are all she needs as she journeys this way
To be a kind person, loyal and true
With patience, integrity, and reliable too
A modern day Ruth is filled full with gratitude
and love
In response to her Redeemer and his sacrificial
love.